BY
PRAYER
AND
FASTING

Bishop Dr. Godfrey K. Tabansi

Bishop Dr. Godfrey K. Tabansi

ISBN-0977861023

Unless otherwise indicated, all scripture references are to the King James Version of the Holy Bible.

The Bible is more current than tomorrow's newspaper. Read it to be wise.

Bishop Dr. Godfrey K. Tabansi

Dedication
I dedicate this book to God who has made
lots of investments into my life.

BY PRAYER AND FASTING

20   And they Brought him unto him (JESUS): and when he saw him, straightway the spirit tare him; and he fell on the ground, and wallowed foaming.

21   And he asked the Father, how long is it ago since this came unto him? And he said of a child.

22   And ofttimes it hath cast him into the fire, and into the waters, to destroy him: but if thou canst do any thing, have compassion on us, and help us.

MARK 9:20-22

INTELLIGENT CONVULSIONS

The Convulsion that troubled the boy in this account was specific in times and places. It chose to embarrass the little boy and his father. In the presence of fire or a large body of water, like a river, the convulsion began. And the convulsions appeared usually so intelligent that, of all places, they often propelled the boy in the direction of danger. The convulsions were, in fact, so expert that they not merely targeted the boy in that direction, they hurled him into the very danger.

Could the boy have been manipulating those events to his own detriment? Could he have been pulling up a "show"? Was it merely some nervous reactions? NO. There was a malevolent intelligence behind those events, for the crisis often chose the rightly identified the crisis as originating in a spirit, an unfriendly demon spirit.

In other cases, such demon spirits of

death and suicide choose other kinds of danger into which they hurl their victims. They could provoke a convulsion, sometimes, in the middle of a person's attempt to run across a busy road with speeding cars and trucks. Unless God intervenes, an accident occurs, only for ignorant men to blame it either on the carelessness of the pedestrian victims of the recklessness of the unfortunate driver.

TELEGULDED "ACCIDENTS"

While a sick man in Washington D.C., the account was narrated to a wealthy man who had died some years back. He had been involved in a motor accident. While he was being rushed to the hospital in a different vehicle, there was a second accident. He was transferred again into another car. Still on the way to the hospital, there was a third crash. The man did not survive the third accident. He died. His corpse was transferred all the same into a forth car, still headed for the hospital. From then, there wasn't another accident. The dead had been done. Were those accidents true "accidents"? No. They were the product of an "Evil Intelligent." Even though they took an appearance they could have put the blame on the driver or some 'mechanical' fault.

WHY THE CONVULSION

Why does the devil do this? The same scripture offers the satanic motive for those coordinated "accidents". From first hand the Father could say to Jesus, "And often times it hath cast him into the fire and in the waters, to destroy him" (v. 22). That was Satan's goal: to destroy the boy, which in fact, is his mission on earth (John 10:10). It did not matter how he went about it, whether by means of fire or water as long as the goal was achieved. It was Mission Accomplished.

Unlike the matter of this boy, the goal may not be the destruction of lives in every case. The goal could be a destruction of finances, a destruction of the home, career, ministry, and so on. If Satan cannot kill a person, the goal usually is to "kill" everything around that person's finances, businesses, health, etc. So that living becomes worse than death and the grave becomes strangely preferable. That was the case with Job and Elijah. When Satan realized that he could not get at Job, he got at Job's business empire, Job's health, with vengeful fury.

IN THE ENVIRONMENT
OF PRAYER

The devils in this category of operation often react strongly in the environment of prayers. Everything remains "normal", even perfect until such persons begin a certain kind of prayer and fasting; then all kinds of "convulsions" break loose from every corner, against them, to discourage and distract them. In the case of the little boy in question, as soon as Jesus came on the scene, the same destructive convulsions commenced.

A person not so spiritually perceptive might have been tempted to conclude that since those convulsion often occurred in environment of danger, Jesus Himself had to be a dangerous hypocrite for His presence to have generated the same kind of phenomenon which was common around fires and waters. The truth, however, was that, that was different kind of convulsion. It was the convulsions to end all convulsions. The spirits of death were reacting to the danger that even confronted their dangerous persons.

DIVINE THERAPY

How does one deal with this "kind" or category of 'strategic" spirits? Jesus said, "THIS KIND" [notice the words "this kind"] can come forth by NOTHING but by "prayer and fasting" (v.29).

Mathew appears to have put that a little more strongly:....this kind goeth not out but by prayer and fasting". (Mathew 17:21)

If you have malaria, the doctor might recommend chloroquine or any of the other anti-malarial drugs to treat that 'kind' of ailment. If you had infections on your skin, he or she might recommend antibiotics—not chloroquine because drugs are specific in the "kind" of category of ailments they are supposed to treat. When the frustrated disciples wondered to Jesus why their orthodox approach to the problem had been futile, Jesus pointed out to them that they were dealing with a unique "kind" of spirit:

and that merely taking tablets was not going
to   help   them.

 Jesus   the   Specialist   Consultant,   then
notified them that the kind of spirit they had
been dealing with could be attacked not
merely with prayers alone or fasting alone,
but by prayer compounded or mixed with
prayer reinforced with, fasting.

How long one takes a drug does not
determine how soon the person gets well. In
fact, the wrong drug can result in a new kind
of complication. How long one has prayed
or been prayed for might neither be
sufficient therapy in dealing with 'strategic'
spirits.

One has to follow the right and proper
prescription.   COMBINE   prayer   with
fasting.   Everyone can fast and pray, so
everyone can deal with those spirits, if the
Great   Physician's   prescription   for   this
"kind" of condition is obeyed. It may take
different people to combine fasting with
prayer and get relief. But relief is
guaranteed. The same "kind" of drug or
medicine can be manufactured by different
pharmaceutical companies, each company

affixing a brand identity to their products. In spite of the different brand names, however, all the drugs or medicines in that category, because they have the same basic components, can treat about the same "kind" of ailments, depending, to some degree on the specific "kind" and stage of disease being treated, and the relative potency of the specific drug or medicine. In the same way, you do not have to wait for the "prayer and the fasting" manufactured by the Bishops prayer cynical company. If thou may actually be very potent. But God has also given you information on the basic components for the manufacturing the same drug.

Not only does He give that vital information, He grants you the license, freely, to do so. Your own bread of the 'drug" may take a day or two longer than the Bishops; but, it will be effective also. And, it is helpful to know how to begin to manufacture one's own drug for oneself.

FASTING FOR GOD'S HEALING AND HONORS

The story of prophet Daniel teaches us another important principle concerning fasting. Daniel and his three friends were taken from Jerusalem to Babylon as captives. King Bebuchadnezzar turned these Hebrew boys over to his assistants to prepare them for service in his government.

This preparation included eating the King's "choice food" (Daniel 1:5), which Daniel refused to eat (4:8). Why? Because doing so would cause him to violate God's law by eating food that the law prohibited or that had been defiled by being part of pagan rituals.

So Daniel and his three friends enters a partial fast. They, did not fast from food altogether, just from the King's assistant to feed them vegetables and water for ten days, and then test them (vv.12-13)

Daniel was taking a big risk, because if the plan failed, not only the King's assistant, but all of them, could have been put to death for displeasing King Bebuchadnezzer. But Daniel was determined to honor God's Word as revealed in His law, and his fast was part of that Commitment. Daniel was trusting God to Honor him in return. God did honor Daniel's Commitment. "at the end of ten days their appearance seemed better and they were fatter than all the youth who had been eating the King's choice food" (Daniel 1:15).

God also gave them a bonus for honoring Him: "As for these four youths, God gave them knowledge and intelligence in every branch of literature and wisdom; Daniel even understood all kinds of visions and dreams" (v.17)

For Daniel, the issue was clear. He knew what Gods's Word taught concerning clean and defiled food, so his decision was not hard to make. He knew that to eat less and obey God was better than to eat more and disobey God. So he fasted from the King's food, trusting God to bring about the desired physical result.

SIDE EFFECTS

One last word. As you begin to administer this prescription, expect some reactions, which might tend to suggest that the worse was getting worse, rather then improving. Like the boy whose case was referred to Jesus, you might experience a tearing, a falling to the ground and a wallowing and foaming in the month (v.20). Do not be deterred by these "alarming" side effects.

The therapy is taking effect. This is the point at which many give up. Thus failing to complete their prescription. They lose benefit even of the mutual medications, and their case becomes more resistant because the devils return with seven other spirits more wicked then themselves (Luke 11:24-26).

A similar situation is reported in Jeremiah 14:17-18, of a people whose commencement of steps towards spiritual cleanliness generated such apparent side effects that they fled back into their previous filth. Hear them"

17   We will burn incense to the 'Queen of Heaven: [The Moon] and sacrifice to her just as much as we like just as we and our fathers before us, and our Kings and prince have always done for in those days we had plenty to eat and we were; well off and happy!

18   But ever since we quit burning incense to the "Queen of Heaven" and stopped worshipping her, we have been in great trouble and have been destroyed by sword and famine (Living Bible).

They gave up on their spiritual medication when the devils that had been afflicting them began to react to their therapy of righteousness, in their repentance from idolatry. That side effect, to them, was a threatening contradiction. They gave up and lapsed back into their melody of idolatry.

Watch out when that begins to happen. Such reaction should not be taken to mean that things are getting worse for all your prayers and fasting.

It is only a sign that things have begun to improve. Hold on more strongly then, for that would be Satan's one last convulsion, before you change status and become the latest sample of God's great intervention.

AMEN.

For any information, please Contact Bishop Dr. Godfrey K. Tabansi at Gods World Christian Ministry/Divine Publishers, Inc.: 240-455-2865
Email: divinepublishersinc@gmail.com

Other Books by
Bishop Dr. Godfrey K. Tabansi

Guiding Your Children Into Their Destiny

Hitting The Target In Soul Winning
(Coming Fall 2015)

Write Your Prayer

Bishop Dr. Godfrey K. Tabansi

www.ingramcontent.com/pod-product-compliance
Lightning Source LLC
Chambersburg PA
CBHW060607030426
42337CB00019B/3649